The Journey Through My Heart

Part II

Sara Sheehan

moonsoulchild

moonsoulchild

moonsoulchild

moonsoulchild

You tried and tried

to show your love,

but they took until you had no more to give.

They never saw you for the beauty you could be.

Instead,

they saw you as the mess you were,

within the mess they've made.

You were never enough for them,

even though you've proven

you're everything they need.

Don't lose sleep,

trying to keep them awake.

Don't drain,

what's left of your energy

trying to revive theirs.

Someone who treats you like an option

won't ever make you a priority.

Stop searching for love,

within lovers who aren't around to love you.

Stop trying to find reasons to stay

when all the signs are telling you go.

You'll never find love,

within unreciprocated love

it doesn't exist.

Just like love within someone else

won't ever exist until you learn to love yourself.

moonsoulchild

Everyone struggles with self-love,

because when self-doubt takes over

it seems more powerful.

Self-doubt is,

your brain throwing curve balls,

trying to disturb your peace.

Rise above the doubts,

the demons trying to make

loving yourself seem powerless.

Loving yourself is magic.

Always love with everything, no holding back.

Sometimes loving intensely

ends in heartache.

Things don't always happen the way we hope,

sometimes forever ends

way sooner than you've hoped.

If you've gave all you could,

And loved with everything

nothing can break you.

moonsoulchild

Quit letting toxic actions of others
preoccupy you into believing
your heart deserves to be cold,
after dealing with their cold tendencies.

Toxic people,
will fill you up
with expectations.
Just to knock you down
with disappointments,
it's **not** you.

You'll meet someone

who will find beauty in your flaws.

Not only within your flaws

but within your scars.

Your past is just a reflection

of the person you used to be,

not the person you're becoming.

Not everyone you love

will love you the same way you love them.

Some will

take advantage of your love.

Some will

only love you enough

to keep your love around.

When your heart is gold,

everyone wants some.

Not everyone wants to reciprocate.

Stop letting your heart

have open availability to ones

who come and go

and come back when they please.

Plant your love within those

who will help you grow

not ones who stunt your growth.

moonsoulchild

Falling in love with yourself

is terribly hard when you know your flaws

downfalls and what you wish to change.

Compared to falling in love with someone,

they love the parts you view as flawed.

That's the beauty in love,

finding someone who helps you

see the beauty in you.

Letting go

"*is one of the hardest things*"

you planted in your head.

Letting go is beautiful,

especially when it's become toxic to you.

Letting go of the old

and welcoming the happiness behind the misery.

Love,

real love,

will surprise you at the time you least expect it.

You won't be looking for it,

it will show up ready to reciprocate the same energy.

Nothing will feel more right,

love that love with everything

that's the love that *deserves* you.

Never lose sight

on being the most important person in your life.

There will be times

you'll forget who you are

putting the needs of others before you.

You can't take care of them

if you're not taking care of you.

You won't love to your full potential

without setting the foundation.

Self-love is,

every loss at loving anyone who made it hard.

It's getting hurt time after time.

You thought your love was enough

to heal anyone you tried

making understand your worth.

It's getting broken down

just to show

the most important person above all,

is *yourself.*

Know the difference,

between love

and love that only lives within you.

Love you hold may be toxic to you

because it's not being reciprocated.

A toxic love

can blind you into opening your eyes

to what real love is like.

moonsoulchild

It's crazy what happens to us

when we believe someone is the one

and fall into love that ends up unrequired love.

It's hard to see through someone when we love them

not just them,

but of the idea of who they could be.

moonsoulchild

Never let your heart turn cold

you owe it to yourself to keep loving.

Being cold will only bring you pain

find the warmth in your heart.

Your love deserves to be felt

you have too much heart to be cold

just because you live in a world

that's *afraid to show their heart*.

moonsoulchild

People fear you most when you love yourself

as if it's some kind, of weapon.

Self-love is

supposed to be the time

most celebrated,

instead you lose

a lot you wish you could've held onto.

moonsoulchild

The universe has a way

of sending you good karma

even at the worst times.

Times which you may question

due to the circumstances.

That's the crazy part,

you never know

when something life changing can happen,

it comes down to you

deciding whether to take the risk.

moonsoulchild

When you find what brings out the fire in you

and what keeps your soul alive

everything will make sense.

Don't go searching,

it's best for what's meant for you

to present to you

even if you don't see it at first.

It's important to make sense of the burdens

to love the blessings.

moonsoulchild

Letting go,

of someone you thought you knew

makes pain surface

when you obsess the idea

of who you loved them to be

not for who they are.

You become attached to the idea

that love would revive

like when you felt it the first time

or how it was never real in the first place.

moonsoulchild

A love that's real,
won't ever change
or outgrow you.

A love that's real,
will grow with you
it won't ever make you believe
you don't deserve it

Love can be blinding

when it comes to years of knowing

and growing with someone.

We condition ourselves to believe

love overpowers everything

forgetting people change

as well as creating toxic behavior.

And sometimes,

we get that confused with love.

moonsoulchild

Your fear is just *self-doubt*

trying to confuse your mind

it's not possible to be free.

Your worries,

are just thoughts created

to convince yourself,

that fear lives within you.

The worries which reside

are just roadblocks hindering you

from *the beauty of you being free*.

Real love doesn't drop out of the sky

real love can't be forced

it takes time.

Sadly, a lot of lost time,

love lost, and pieces that will always be broken.

Those pieces are pieces you've outgrown

which makes room

for the love that's meant to grow.

You can't give yourself to anyone if you're broken

each piece can't be given separately

expecting someone to complete you.

Become whole on your own

put the pieces of you back together

than you'll be able to share your love with someone.

It's so beautiful

seeing people happy

and *self-love* written all over them.

I think it's beautiful

when someone is growing

into the soul they're meant to bloom into.

Self-love will always be

the most important lesson in your story.

moonsoulchild

You grow connections with people

you'll never believe you'd connect with

which makes it harder in the end

when you need let them go.

People change,

and it's hard to believe people grow.

The outcome isn't always growing together

but growing apart.

moonsoulchild

Let people grow, don't hold them back from becoming who they are destined to be. When you met them, where they were wasn't where they were headed. Keep in mind, people change, and it's wrong for you to hold them inside boundaries where growth is a burden. We love people for who they are when the love first sparked, without thinking there is room for change. We become adapted to who they are in that moment, without realizing how beautiful they will blossom into one day because

we're afraid to let go of who they once were.

Self-love is

the hardest chapter in your life to uncover.

There is so many dimensions

to loving every part of you.

Accepting your flaws

and how they tie into your beauty.

Letting go of old habits

that created toxic behavior.

Bringing in the new

the growth, and lastly, the **love**.

People think as soon as you find *self-love*

you'll be endlessly happy.

Self-love is loving yourself

through every wall

you never had the courage to knock down.

It's days full of happiness,

and days full of self-doubt.

Loving yourself is a beautiful disaster all in one.

moonsoulchild

Always love more

never hold back your love

because some may not be ready for it.

You'll never regret loving more,

you'll only regret the love you should of gave

when you didn't give your all.

Ego driven souls

could never give you what you need to fulfill you.

Everything would be a competition

between who's right or who's wrong

forgetting about the love

that's shared between the two.

Love is lost when it comes

to *their ego over loving you.*

Falling in love with someone

based on who they are

and how they make you feel

is a love that's true.

Falling in love with someone

because you're lonely

and the idea

will only bring you pain.

Don't force falling into love

it's a beautiful miracle when it finds you.

moonsoulchild

Self-love is

and will always be

the biggest struggle we face throughout our lives.

Struggling loving ourselves through our eyes

because we place our energy

trying to be loved by someone else.

The only love fulfilling

is love from within

until then, no love will feel enough.

The scariest thing

is giving your all away to someone and
expecting them to give you the same in return. Not
knowing until it is too late, when feelings resonated
and you are deep in. You will love the worst kinds of
hearts throughout your lifetime, but one thing, you
will love these people for a reason, there is always a
purpose. Not everyone will be someone meant to
stay, when the bad takes itself out the story, stop
blaming yourself. Stop thinking it is your fault such
tragedy happened, which was not you're doing in the

first place. You gave all of you, you showed up, gave way more than you received. Remember those times. The times you loved and did everything, those are important. Not their character, not the way they treated you. You'll end up exactly where they want you by hoarding the pain they left you with. Do not run from the signs when you see them, accept sometimes people disappear from your life only for a blessing to appear. The universe will never take something away from you without giving you something much more beautiful. Let go of what is gone.

Never change your heart because you
lessened your worth
for someone who doesn't even know theirs.

moonsoulchild

Those who take advantage

are ones who know they can take without

having to give, ones who are not worthy of any piece

of your heart that you have, to give. Anyone who

leaves should not get another chance to rekindle your

love, because your love was too intense for them in

the first place. Some people do not deserve second

chances. Second chances do not exist to ones who do

not care about intentionally hurting you. Start

planting love within those who help you grow, not

ones who stunt your growth and leave you confused

as to why you loved them in the first place. There is no reason to hold love towards them when they have never loved you enough to hold onto you, or whether they loved you at all. Stop attaching ideas that love exists in souls who only drain you from thinking your heart is not meant to love. Stop giving the wrong ones the parts of you only the right one should receive.

Not everyone you love is someone who deserves it.
Some are just a lesson,
and that one after every lesson, will be a blessing.

It's a beautiful thing,

to love who you are and not give that love up.

It's a beautiful thing,

to be able to give yourself

the same effort you put into everyone else.

moonsoulchild

I believe we have multiple *soul-mates* in our lifetime,

not just as relationships

but as friendships also.

I believe you shouldn't overlook

any hold someone has over your soul, explore it.

But also, know not every soul-mate will stay,

some just show their purpose and go.

44

moonsoulchild

It's so frightening to wear your heart on your sleeve

to always follow your heart.

It's the scariest thing in the world

to give your most intimate parts to someone

when you might lose that love one day.

I pray whatever is holding you

from being genuinely happy,

passes quickly and you learn how important it is

to love yourself

with *every piece of you that feels broke*n.

moonsoulchild

It's exhausting

having a heart that's always taken for granted.

It's exhausting

trying to prove my love time and time again

just to become disappointed at the outcome.

Life is all about moments.

That's why it's important

to live fiercely within every moment.

That one moment

could turn into the rest of your life.

moonsoulchild

"*The grass isn't always greener on the other side*"

doesn't mean you have to stay

on the side the grass doesn't grow.

moonsoulchild

I pray you wake up today and see the beauty you
have been searching for within everyone else. I pray
you wake up today and understand your worth,
because it was never anyone's job to show you how
beautiful you truly are, but you.

Sometimes we see others

in ways we don't see ourselves.

That's the beauty in loving someone,

you see them for everything they are

and love them for exactly that, flaws, scars, and all.

Dead ends,

aren't always the end

sometimes they're just roadblocks

trying to convince you

that something more beautiful

isn't waiting for you at the end.

Don't let that stop you from finding what you deserve.

I know how hard it can be

to set yourself free from *toxic* energy.

But I promise you, once you do

it's like a breath of fresh air.

Putting your energy where it's only reciprocated

will have you on cloud nine.

Which results in,

    the best decision you could ever make.

moonsoulchild

It's crazy,

how people can come into your life

at the darkness times

and bring the light you've been searching for.

Those are the ones who matter most

not to help pick up the pieces

but instead,

they're the missing piece.

Stop imagining what life would be like

with someone who treats you like you deserve.

Stop wondering how happy you'd be

letting someone in.

Don't be scared to give love a chance

even though it can be the craziest ride, it's all worth it.

True happiness is worth everything.

Not every relationship,

can be fixed

don't let anyone make you feel

like you're wrong for walking away

instead of trying to save the love

that's no longer felt like love,

because it's became toxic.

Some things aren't meant to be recovered.

Some people,

don't know what they have until they lose it.

Some people don't know the beauty of the other side

until they break free

from what's holding them back from it.

moonsoulchild

It's sad seeing beautiful souls

take back the same people who hurt them.

That's where you'll always go wrong

leave the past where it's at

recovering it will only keep the pain alive.

You'll never truly be happy.

The saddest part of all,

people don't think they have the strength
to leave toxic relationships.
Instead of making excuses why you can't
put that effort into why you should.
So many people find reasons to stay
rather than reasons to go
that's where you'll always go wrong.

moonsoulchild

Go ghost,

nothing does more damage than silence.

Sometimes it brings us peace.

moonsoulchild

You should never forget,

who you are when you love someone

it's always you first

the love they give you only can add to that

not take away from who you are.

Don't ever let anyone

make you believe what you feel is wrong.

You're capable of feeling, without a time limit.

Love is timeless.

Happiness is timeless.

Don't let others make you believe

you shouldn't be ready

for the blessings coming your way.

Don't be afraid

to let go of ties that were loose for some time.

Don't be afraid

to embrace the change that will make life beautiful.

Finding the one doesn't happen overnight,

it doesn't happen as soon as you pray.

But once you pray,

your prayer is listened to

and the universe aligns the one

and puts them on their path to find you.

Just understand,

you'll need to know who's not meant for you,

to know who is.

moonsoulchild

Don't stop searching for your soul mate.

Don't give up.

You'll go through a lot of countless disappointments

to find them, but the search will be worth it.

Once you let go of the bitterness of past loves

and embrace the reciprocated love

you'll see the worth.

Loving yourself,

not only brings confidence

it brings strength to love another

with the same kind of love you give yourself,

without taking away

from the love you have for yourself.

Self-love is beautiful, you should try it today.

moonsoulchild

It's important to always surround yourself

with people who want to see you succeed.

Surrounding yourself

with people who are always in competition

will only make you feel as if you're not good enough.

Don't settle for anyone

who makes it seem like you're hard to love.

Don't be afraid to be vulnerable.

It's important to feel every emotion

stop treating your heart bad

because you've always gave too much

and always loved too much.

Those are beautiful traits

just not everyone deserves them.

Don't give up, someone will feel it.

Stop blaming your heart

for the countless times you've been hurt.

Stop turning to heartless behavior

to shield you from being broken.

You're making it difficult to find love meant for you.

Not everyone is going to love you,

but your heart will always love.

Your *self-love* journey.

is the most important story you'll live to tell.

It's not a fairytale world

you'll find yourself with your emotions

all over the place, you're human.

But you've found the beauty in yourself,

and conquered loving yourself through every flaw.

Stop chasing love

that isn't attached to your growth.

Stop latching onto outcomes

that only leave you bruised.

Follow your heart,

go all in, but never overlook the signs.

When something doesn't feel right, believe it.

Don't stay because you're comfortable

follow the spark.

moonsoulchild

Falling in love with someone,

you had no intentions on falling for

is the most beautiful kind of love.

No forcing chemistry or trying to save them.

Just a pure, raw connection, that *created on its own*.

If you've yet to experience

love with another person, don't go searching for it.

Find the love within yourself,

set the foundation

of what you wish to be reciprocated.

Watch the universe start aligning

than your one will come.

But it starts with loving you.

moonsoulchild

We live in a world

where everyone wants love

but accepts toxicity and unrequited love.

I've seen more people expressing sadness

when it comes to people

who are deeply in love.

Everyone wants love

but has no idea what love is

because they're too busy drowning in misery.

Some people will enter your life

and leave for the same reason, it's their purpose.

Then someone will enter your life

and show you how beautiful it is

to let things develop naturally.

Witnessing how beautiful it is,

to fall in love with your best friend.

We all have bad days.

Don't let bad days

cloud your mind with the thought

you won't ever be happy.

You need to find the balance between both

each will help you understand

how important it is to love yourself.

Loving yourself,

through the good and the bad

you'll feel invincible.

moonsoulchild

Don't believe anyone

when they say falling in love is scary.

People say this because being hurt

is the only outcome painted in their mind.

Falling in love,

is one of the purest feelings in the world

you feel incredible

moonsoulchild

Stop fearing the unknown,

stop fearing what could happen

do what you love, take chances

Life's too short to analyze what could go wrong.

moonsoulchild

You live to take chances,

you don't live to worry the outcome.

You could miss the moment of your life

that could make your whole future

fearing what could go wrong.

Live a little,

live on the edge,

love with your whole heart.

nothing could ever break you.

moonsoulchild

Protecting your heart

doesn't mean become heartless.

There's nothing beautiful in having "no heart"

Stop treating your heart bad

because of the hurt you had repeated.

Stop treating your heart as if it's not there

it's the most *powerful piece of you*.

moonsoulchild

When you force any kind of relationship

with anyone that's not meant

to go on any longer

it will only result in more hurt.

Stop letting hurt grow within situations

you should of let go.

Stop holding onto what they've already let go.

moonsoulchild

If you get lucky enough

to create a beautiful friendship with someone, then

fall in love with them

don't let them go.

That's the purest kind of love you'll find

someone who's a friend to you,

someone who loves you unconditionally,

someone who falls in love with you too.

moonsoulchild

Love is beautiful when it's not forced,

the connection becomes

an unbreakable bond

the chemistry is out this world

and the sex is phenomenal.

Love created off a friendship

is something more than a relationship,

it's a *soulmate*.

moonsoulchild

I've tried saving people for years,

tried making them see

my love could heal them from their hurt.

To the point I was trying to make them love me.

I couldn't save someone

and expect them to reciprocate the same love,

that's all the relationship becomes based on.

moonsoulchild

I used to be the "*sad girl*"

I used it as my excuse

to blame love for the countless mistakes I made.

Choosing to be involved

with people who proved

why I should of chose to walk instead.

I chose my heart because love was important

having someone love me was important

love was my motivation

unfortunately,

I forgot to condition that love.

I accepted love from some that were not whole.

I accepted love from some

who chose to love me when I was convenient.

I accepted love from some who chose

to love me in private

while showcasing me as the bad guy to the world.

moonsoulchild

I accepted all forms of love.

I chose to stay around to fix some.

I chose to try and move forward

from the hurt some caused

and give a second chance when it was not deserved.

I chose to forgive

instead of holding grudges

which would only hurt me in the end.

I chose to settle.

I chose to stay where I felt familiar,

because starting over was scary.

Comfort felt good.

I chose to settle even after my heart

tried to tell me countless times,

there was more.

I looked away from the signs.

I chose to be blind.

I chose to hold on when it was best

for me to let go.

I chose many things that led me to pain

but I never chose love

because I always felt love,

moonsoulchild

it was never a decision whether I loved

love was always alive within me.

I never had to chose to love,

I loved everyone even if they hurt me.

I loved even when it wasn't reciprocated.

I loved even when I let go.

Love was never a choice

I couldn't help but to love.

When someone says "loves a choice"

I think of a switch-if love's a choice,

and you choose who you love,

you can just decide to not love?

you can choose to not feel love?

that's where it gets me.

I chose so many things because I love

I also chose to let go of many because of love.

none of this would be anything,

if I didn't *feel.*

moonsoulchild

I *pray you find* someone

who matches your energy

and soul

the exact amount needed

to fulfill that missing piece.

Before you find them,

I pray you find you.

Note to self

To witness you grow into the woman you are, to see
the changes first hand has been incredible. Being the
girl who never spoke up when things did not settle
right with your spirit, to destroying any wrong idea of
who you are labeled to be. Some may have seen you
as shy, unable to forth come the imitated soul you
were made out to be, because who you were was far
different than the "someone everyone was". Your
heart was always big, you did everything you could, *to
show your heart and the love you held*, to the world.

moonsoulchild

When I found love, real love, true love,

I never felt the same comfort

I felt when I was in relationships

that were not growing more than they were.

I felt bursts of happiness from the moment I woke up,

to the minute I closed my eyes.

When you find love, real love,

every day feels like the honeymoon phase.

The disagreements, arguments,

the misunderstandings

won't change the love,

it just adds balance to the relationship.

I feared comfort once I realized

I settled because it was familiar,

not because it made me happy.

The spark that started the flame

never let it go out

because comfort became more familiar.

Don't get lazy when it comes to loving someone

you don't want to live without.

moonsoulchild

My love shined too bright

to heal anyone I've loved

my job wasn't to heal them

but to love them enough.

But when I discovered

the love became lost,

I became lost too.

moonsoulchild

I couldn't blame my heart

for loving what was for me,

even when it came to hurting people in the process.

I never intentionally

wanted to bring pain upon anyone.

But I've learned,

blessings will appear

even at the darkest times.

It wasn't my job to block the light I deserved.

moonsoulchild

In my past,

every time I thought I was in love

I came to realization

that love wasn't love if I had to chase for it.

It wasn't love if I had to prove my worth.

I stepped away

from wanting to find love

within people who didn't have love to give me,

that's when love found me.

Everyone I loved, I chased.

I tried convincing them my love was for them.

I knew the love I had to give,

was a love that could heal anyone from hurt.

I was made to love

I got that confused with loving

anyone who made it easy,

when the love was only conditioned by me.

moonsoulchild

Sadness did not consume my life in a whole. Sadness would come and go, more so in waves, then it chose to stay more often than I anticipated. Now, happiness has came into my life to stay, I have parted ways with my dark days. Those dark days are far behind me, as all I'm left with are the memories of broken promises, broken dreams, and disappointments of false hopes. I let sadness consume me of my time. I let sadness consume me of my energy. I let sadness become my reality. Sadness contained most of my memory, As I only told stories about lovers who spoke more than they have ever set action to. I wrote stories how my love was too intense for anyone who touched my heart. I was too much of a woman back then, I was too much of a wholesome lover, to ever be loved back then. No one in my past was ready for my love. The kind of love I gave, was the kind of love the moon gave the night sky, the way it lit through the darkness. I guess what I'm saying is, my love shined too bright to heal anyone I have loved, because my job was not to heal them, my job was to love them, love them enough in order to find the piece of me within them. The piece of me that added to the story of finding me. It might sound selfish, to pick up missing pieces within lovers, old friends, and old flames, but I have come to understand, there is a piece of us in everyone we have a connection with, and those pieces add to our story. Every disappointment, I have paid my dues. I have written my wrongs within everyone I disappointed. Everyone who has done me wrong, I forgave. Everyone I did wrong, I let them go. No one I ever hurt was intentional, and truly, my heart would never hurt the one I love, that is just the way the story played out. Maybe I never loved you the way my heart needed in the first place, but I sure loved you in ways that made sense until our story ended. I accepted, people were written into our lives, and to never question the intention, to be open to love, be open to understand

the purpose of the love that surfaced in the first place.
I, never forgot the love I held for ones I let free, to this
day I still hold love within my heart for ones who
planted their seed within my heart but never grew,
because, for some reason, it was not meant to. At the
time I never knew the love would not grow, I did not
know our story would end slow. That is the scariest
part, as I reflect on my life, I find myself wondering
where I went wrong with one's I thought I would hold
close to my heart. I realized it was never my fault,
whether I was done wrong, or it was my wrong doing,
the universe knew that love was not the kind of love
my heart could handle, because it was only out to
destroy me. I picked up the pieces many times, within
lovers who let me give more than they wished to
reciprocate. I had lovers who never gave but loved to
watch me drain my love to consume them. I had
lovers who loved me back, but never loved me
enough. As I say, loved me back, but never enough,
there was always more for me. I had too much heart,
to give someone half. I had too much heart, to let
someone think it was right to only reciprocate half

their love, while watching me drain myself to become
someone of their need.

I picked up the pieces many times.

I watched myself fall apart as I fixed them.

I tried saving them, while completely losing myself.

My heart survived.

I cried a thousand times.

I became a fool to everyone I let love me

but somehow I made myself out to be the bigger one.

That's the thing, about people with good hearts, we
always give more, without realizing the importance of
getting the same energy reciprocated. Having a good
heart is dangerous, because you find yourself in the
circle of unrequited love. That's when I learned, just
because you love someone, doesn't mean you are
meant to. Just because you love someone doesn't
mean they are someone you need to keep in your life.
Sometimes you need to love someone enough to let
them go. People will take until you have no more to
give. There's no fixing them, there's no making
anyone understand what your love's like.

moonsoulchild

After all the hurt, all the time you wasted trying to rekindle love that set the flame to fire, as you slowly watch that fire burn out. A real one, will walk into your life, and they will feel it. You will feel it, nothing will be said. Happiness will consume you like sadness never could, it will love you in ways sadness couldn't. Let happiness be your light. Let happiness plant that seed within your heart and let it grow this time. Because now, I loved myself enough to let go of everything that consumed me of me, as I watch the old me fade into the background, I watch the new version of me become the woman I dreamed to be. I will let happiness take control of my life, my dark days are over. Sadness, I know you'll always find a way back in, but I will never let you stay, I will never let you consume me of making me believe people who do not really deserve me, have any right loving me in ways they could never amount to. Sadness, I know it is time, we say our goodbyes, I just want you to know, having someone who loves me back is incredible, more than chasing someone who never loved me ever could be. I'm tired of trying to show my heart to ones

who do not deserve the time, while I can give my
heart to someone who appreciates my time. I was lost
for a long time, but I connected with me again, and
happiness and me, we are a thing. It is time, to say
goodbye, you consumed me of too much time,
thinking I was blind, thinking I was not enough, but
listen, you were just another fool, I was made out to
be the bigger one when I thought you'd fill me up
with your remedy. This time, the jokes on you, I'm too
good for you.

Sadness, you're now in the rearview mirror,

I have no vision of you.

Hello happiness, *I'm so ready for you.*

moonsoulchild

The one thing,

I always wish I had a better understanding of

was letting go.

When I loved someone, I loved them, wholeheartedly.

There wasn't anything I wouldn't do for them.

I always put all of me in every time

even if it left me with nothing.

I never analyzed the outcome

or whether there was one

I took the risk. I loved everyone I let close to me

for a reason, whether they're still apart of my life

or we went different paths, I loved them, their love

was essential to me. Their love was important to me.

At that moment of my life I needed it. Within the

moment, loving these people felt right, at that time I

never thought the outcome could be me looking

back. At that time, I never would of thought I'd be

loving anyone else, but I know now, that's how my

heart loves, there's no other way. I have an

understanding people enter our lives for reasons, and sometimes they don't last in our story. Learning to let go wasn't the easiest lesson, there's still friends I still hold close to my heart because loving them too close was too hard, it didn't change my love for them. My heart beats hard to the point it could make some uncomfortable if they're not familiar with that kind of love. My heart longed for more, which some couldn't reciprocate. My heart needed balance, it needed security, it needed its twin flame, unfortunately, none of the ones from my past made the cut. Everyone from my past was a reflection of the love I needed to let go of. Letting go has been the biggest lesson, there's so many people I let go that I thought I'd grow old loving, but I conditioned my heart to hold these people close to me because I was too afraid to lose them. I wasn't prepared to lose them, I wasn't ready to let go of everything I once knew, everything that was once comfort to me. I took comfort as a rest stop and hide from the more I could be, the more I could love. I let myself become afraid to be freely who I am because I let people put me inside boundaries they accepted. I let myself be loved conditionally from people who only needed me for their advantage. I let myself become an option to those I made a priority. I grew up around so much love, and I always dreamed of finding the love that everyone made seem so beautiful.

I searched for love that wasn't love in the end. I searched for love that ended up pain. I searched for love that ended up nothing but a mistake. I searched for love within people who always took more than they gave, and somehow believed love still would remain. I searched my life for love within people I seen something good in, whether they were good for me, or just a good person, I let them love me, how they wished to, as I gave them the love I deserved. I learned to let go once I learned not everyone who loves you stays, some may love you only until they find something better, some might outgrow once you find who you are. Letting go, is the hardest lesson I had to learn, but when I let go of ones who were the closest to me, with feeling how good it made me, I realized letting go doesn't hurt.

moonsoulchild

Letting go saved me from staying in connections that

were leading me nowhere, that's why letting go was

the greatest lesson life taught me.

Letting go brought me blessings,

the love I prayed for all along.

Sometimes you need to stop watering dead plants

And start creating an environment

for new ones to grow within.

moonsoulchild

I always believed love was beautiful,

even through the hurt, disappointment, and constant

search for it. The constant let down when I discovered

the one I was loving, was another lesson. I never gave

up, because I knew love wasn't meant to be any of

these things, I was just letting love live within people I

wasn't meant to love. There were many times I picked

up pieces I should've left broken, but I chose to keep

loving. I refused to believe love wasn't meant to be

beautiful. Through the pain, I always kept love sane. I

always made love something beautiful, even if it was

just within my own story.

moonsoulchild

I refused to believe that love came with hurt, pain, and constant disappointment. People who walked into my life and opened my heart were something special, even if all they brought was pain, I find the beauty in loving them even though they chose to break my heart. I loved and to me, that's all I needed. I never lost sight on how beautiful love was, because I always loved with every part of me and I never let love fail me, love has never failed me. Regardless if pain came with love, or if I conditioned myself to believe being loved with conditions with something that was okay, I learned a lesson. I learned love is love and the way people love me will never be the same as I love them. I will always love the same. I was born to love, I was born to show my heart. I was born to give my all. I was put on this life to love, regardless if I wasn't meant to be loved in return, I never gave up on finding love I was meant to fit with. I was torn apart numerous times, years of trying to understand why I couldn't be loved the same way I loved, I realized there's no one that can love me the way I love.

moonsoulchild

After I stopped analyzing trying to make someone
love me the same, I found someone who loves me the
way I was meant to be loved, the way I deserved to be
loved, after all the time I tried to make love fit in my
heart that wasn't meant to, I let it all go, just to let
your love in, I can't believe all this time your love was
the love I was searching for and now
I finally feel what real love is,

I finally feel it.

moonsoulchild

My heart was fragile

when it was time to open my love

to people whose intentions were unwritten.

I built a wall around my heart

no one was able to break down.

My heart was too soft to be broken

and *too strong to taken advantage of.*

moonsoulchild

I wasn't interested

in being accepted, especially when it came to
a crowd I didn't fit into. I never forced a connection
with people who never felt me. I might have
misunderstood my purpose, I might have chased for
love, but I never made someone feel like I needed
them. I never felt the need of someone like the need
to find myself and love me. I never thought someone
could fill me with the courage to love myself, the way I
could pitch my own voice, and love me with every part
of myself I took for granted. I wasn't interested in
being someone's doormat, but that didn't mean I

never let people stay longer than their time granted, I can't lie and say I didn't try to make things work when they were way overdue to be outgrown. I can't say I never let someone walk all over me and made me believe their love was something I lived and breathed, I kept letting ones open me up just to fail me. I never said I'd give up, sometimes I had too much pride, sometimes I had too much heart, I couldn't give up anything that I promised I'd take to the grave. I couldn't tell you why I chose to let people come and go when it was time to be real. I couldn't tell you why I tried to keep people around who weren't a permanent stay. I couldn't tell you why I thought loving myself wasn't important when it came to letting everyone else touch my heart—I never understood how my love for them could be honest if I couldn't even be real with myself. I never had the same love for myself. The importance of my self-worth was out the window when it came to my worth within lives I held no purpose in. I couldn't tell you why I fought wars with people who spoke on me like I wasn't worthy, but I couldn't stand up for myself because I didn't know my worth. I never said I was confident, when it came to myself, I never knew how important I was because everyone else was more important. I fought love for years trying to understand why no one loved me the same I prayed to be, the whole time I was praying to be loved, but couldn't understand the only way I could be loved, was to condition my love within myself. I stood for much, yet I could never stand for anything when it came to speaking on the love I knew I didn't deserve, but still let consume me. I was weak for so many people, I let them destroy me with their fire, while watching me burn without trying to revive me. I was once the same kind of toxic I was consuming, I never put myself first, I let myself become destroyed, to the point I was almost broken. I never said I didn't think about falling apart, I just thought about the pieces and the amount of time trying to mend myself together. No one had the strength to break me, I take pride in knowing no one has what it takes to make me feel as I'm worth breaking. I wasn't interested in making connections that lead me nowhere. I wasn't interested in putting my heart into something that wouldn't give me a story. I wasn't interested in wasting a moment trying to be understood by someone who couldn't understand. I wasn't interested in being told my worth from people who couldn't even love themselves. It wasn't my thing, to be within a crowd that thought I wouldn't be someone, someone other than a fool, because I know they always saw me being someone, but never someone more than them. To everyone who doubted me, I pray you find your closure within these words, now I'm somebody more than you thought of me. I'm now somebody I knew I would be. To everyone who once played my heart, I pray you find someone who loves you the exact when you need, because I couldn't. I couldn't love someone who made me feel like it was impossible to love myself— because neither could you. To everyone I once loved, I pray you're good. Because I once loved you, but no longer hold that love within me. I'm more than a misunderstood woman who couldn't be felt, who couldn't be loved for who I am, but always loved. To everyone I called a friend, those days were long ago,

moonsoulchild

I'm not saying they aren't remembered, I'm just saying

there's more I wish to forget, than I wish to remember.

I pray you've found your peace,

and the you, you've hoped to be.

To everyone who reads this,

I'm somebody now,

someone I always knew I was

but was terribly scared to be, I cared too much

about what I was made out to be,

than what I loved about me.

I love me now,

I'm not interested

in loving anyone more, than I love me.

moonsoulchild

I was never a fan

of changing who I am

to make others comfortable.

I'd rather you be uncomfortable

for trying to change me.

I highly believe in closure.

I believe you should understand why you left things
the way you did. I don't believe you need to figure
this out within the other person, I believe the closure
should come from you, you need to find the
understanding on why you let them go.

Outgrowing old habits, old friends, old lovers, is a part
of life. Stop thinking growing apart from someone
means the worst outcome. What's already broken,
there's no mending together

what's already gone.

Your love taught me what love is supposed to feel like. Not the assumption of what love is thought to be. You touched me with the kind of love, that leaves an imprint on the heart. The kind of love that can't be forgotten. Your love inspires the fire in me. Your love gives me life. Your love makes me realize no love I've consumed was ever good enough because *you were the dose I needed.*

People are afraid

to let go of toxic situations

because they hold onto

every good memory they have of someone

and attach to it,

thinking the exact feeling will revisit again.

Toxic people are like drugs

having you search for what's gone

while *destroying you slowly in the process*.

moonsoulchild

My past is left in the past

no rekindling it, reliving it, or reminiscing it.

What's gone is gone.

What I outgrew

what outgrew me

is out of sight, out of mind.

I'm looking forward

the future holds something so much more beautiful

than the past could ever give me.

moonsoulchild

We need to start *celebrating*

happiness around us more

we need to start putting

more love into the world

to receive the same blessings in return.

moonsoulchild

Some still may not understand me

some still may hate me

but my soul never poisoned anyone

with anything but love.

I never fit with some people

because I never wanted the same.

I chose to not

become victim of the hype

and created my own.

moonsoulchild

I'm proud of myself

for always being true to myself

even when almost losing myself.

The love I once knew

that had pain written all over it

was re-created into love with purpose.

I sparked the magic in me

when I found inner beauty in the depths of my soul

I haven't chose to focus on anything since.

Everything about me is beautiful

whether I drown in *self-doubt*,

I find myself in the balance of being human.

At the end of every day,

being able to take the day in, reflect

but never let it become a change.

To know, I mastered *loving* me.

You can't fight someone's demons for them

that's why, they're their demons, *not* yours.

You can't make someone feel *not* feel pain.

I tried helping

but it took a toll on my overall mental health.

Love isn't love

when you're trying to save

or fix someone

trying to make someone understand who they are.

It's always important

to take care of you

you won't be able to give someone a piece of you

if you can't appreciate and love you.

Time heals wounds from pain

you must feel, what you feel

and let yourself grow from it.

Follow your heart

but lead with an open mind, you *will always be good.*

moonsoulchild

No one who ever left my life

and came back was meant to stay

they're not here now.

Everyone I let back in was because I chose to let them.

Someone coming back into your life

doesn't mean it's meant to be.

Take in mind,

why did they leave?

why did they come back?

what are their intentions?

your heart can't take all the confusion.

To love myself first,

it was not about how I loved, I knew my heart was big and I was born to love, it was more about giving that same love to myself I gave to some who never reciprocated a piece of that love. I would take care of my heart first. I would love myself first. Love after you find this, does not feel like the love I was chasing. A different kind of love. I feel whole on my own, but they add to my completeness. The love I prayed for, and the love I chased turned out to be different paths. The love I prayed for was love I found within everything decided to overlook about me. The flaws I let define me and make peace with the burdens of the hate for myself. To find the beauty. When love is real, there is no second guessing. Take care of home first. Take care of your soul. Nothing will come from planting love in places it will never grow because you chose to love them before you.

There's a different kind of rawness in understanding you, and the love that comes with it.

moonsoulchild

I've loved and lost

and loved again.

My heart didn't stop loving because I lost.

I kept loving because my heart

didn't deserve to become cold

after all the love I had to give.

I wasn't going to punish my heart

Because I chose to put my heart in the hands

of the ones who never felt me the way I felt them.

My love ran deep,

but it never deep enough

to touch anyone who *wasn't meant to love me*.

Do not hold onto what is not meant to stay. When you find things starting to take up too much space on the side of your heart you keep things you are scared to let go. When the love becomes comfortable. Comfort brings love, but love is supposed to make you feel at home and knowing at any moment it can feel like the first time. Love will test you, it is supposed to balance you, plus what is love without challenging? Loving someone who gives your soul the exact amount of love and the exact amount of comfort. Do not hold on too tight when it comes to ending, because the beginning of the rest of your life could be waiting for you.

When it feels right, explore it.

moonsoulchild

If someone

doesn't nurture your soul

the way your soul should be feed

it's not worth the energy.

Don't let anyone who doesn't bring positivity

towards your growth

anywhere near you.

Once I decided to soul search, love will find me.

As I found love within myself,

someone found love in me.

I always inspired to be me,

I allowed myself to love what loved me.

moonsoulchild

The girl who was blinded in her flaws.
Wanted to be accepted but did not want to be known.
Did not want to be anyone but myself, wanted people
to love me for that, but had no clue what who that
was. All I felt I could give was my heart, so I gave my
love to anyone who thought they could handle it.
Spent a lot of time wasted, playing the waiting game,
or finding out it just was not meant to fit. I put my
heart into everything, and it burned me a lot of times.
Who I loved, the connections I made, are some of the
most defining parts of me. Refusing to look back and

not giving my energy anything that lacks the energy I am currently involved with. What I found has shaped me into the woman I am today. I found peace; within loves I lost. Friends I thought I would grow with, I pray you are growing too. I am at peace with us. At peace with who has entered my life just to tell me they could not stay. At peace with knowing the person who existed before I became whole, is someone I cannot become. I grew too much to let anything which I let go turn everything inside out. The emotions have been gone, but the impact it left on my heart is forever there, so it will always feel real when I write it. but know, it is just a reflection. To everyone who doubted me, I pray you find closure within these words, now I am somebody, somebody more than you thought of me. I am somebody I knew I could be. To everyone who once played my heart, I pray you find someone who loves you for who you are, because I couldn't. I couldn't love someone who made me feel like it was impossible to love myself—because neither could you. To everyone I once loved, I pray you are good. I once loved you, but I no longer hold that love

within me. I am somebody more than a
misunderstood woman who could not be felt, who
could not be loved for who I was, but always
continued to love. To everyone I called a friend, those
days were long ago, I am not saying they are not
remembered, there is just more I wish to forget, than I
wish to remember. I pray you found peace and found
the soul you wish to be. I cared too much about what
I was thought out to be than what I loved about me.
I love me now,

    I'm not interested in loving anyone more
than I love me.

When I fell for someone,

I thought was my soulmate, it took a lot of learning
what love was not, to leave him and know someone
else out there deserved my love. To reflect and
separate the good from the bad, and really think
about who gave more, whether it was reciprocated
and whether it was something I deserved. I realize
now all the signs I should let go long ago.

Do not go back letting it happen again because you
love them, love them enough to let go of the person
you thought they were. Save your heart from hurting
and love yourself more to know your self worth is
more important than trying to be worth anything to
them. Sometimes it is better to love from afar because
loving too closely is too much. Not everyone you love
will be someone you will have in your life forever. It
will hurt. It might bruise, but *time will heal all wounds*,
and you will understand it was just another lesson
how love is still searching for you.

moonsoulchild

The love I once knew

that had pain written all over it

was re-created into love with purpose.

I spent years trying to prove my worth

without knowing what I even deserved.

I spent years loving people who didn't love me back

but still tried making them love me.

I tried to make sense

of why I never found love where pain resided

without realizing I created it.

moonsoulchild

I pray you find the light

that's been hiding behind the darkness.

I pray you realize

there's no love in what's forced or not reciprocated.

I pray you stop

chasing someone that didn't love you.

I pray you find the light

that makes sense of everything

you thought you knew.

There's negativity everywhere

you won't win if you react to everyone

that throws curve balls your way.

To win is to not react

block anything that doesn't bring blessings.

moonsoulchild

Opening your eyes

and seeing the toxic in people

is heartbreaking.

Someone you once loved, still might

finding out their toxic and how incredibly hard

trying to separate the two.

moonsoulchild

Many try saving others

without understanding it's impossible.

You can't save someone from their pain

they need to make peace with their burdens.

Saving someone doesn't equal love

there's no guarantee they'll love you.

Love when you feel it, not to prove you can.

moonsoulchild

How can you take the time

to love someone

when you're spending all the time

trying to help them love themselves

Just because you're born to love,

doesn't mean everyone is someone to love.

Just because you have a connection

doesn't mean you're soulmates.

Just because you gave all you could

and didn't get it reciprocated,

doesn't mean give up.

Love will find you when it's time.

moonsoulchild

you give me peace of mind

you give my heart

the feeling of home

I couldn't have prayed harder

your love is my safe place

- Don't over indulge yourself in any unnecessary pain.

- Don't try to fix what never had the proper foundation.

- Don't try mending together what's already broken.

- Don't try releasing your pain while feeding into where it created

sometimes it's best to walk away.

moonsoulchild

Mental health days are so important.

Spending time in your own solitude

doesn't mean you're depressed

somedays you just need to take a break

from the world and be away

there's *nothing wrong with that.*

moonsoulchild

It's beautiful,

to be a part of someone's life while they're growing.

But how incredible it is

to be a part of someone's *growth*

after all the pain, heartache,

and times where they were lost with no direction.

moonsoulchild

You can't always blame others

for the way they treat you

when you're the one allowing them to.

maybe you're the toxic one

If you can't ever admit to being wrong

and holding *toxic* traits from the past

letting them shape you,

how are you supposed to *grow*?

moonsoulchild

we make *love* so intense

the passion runs so wild

we end up in a different *universe*.

that's how crazy our love is.

I never believed in fairytales

never dreamt of the "perfect" wedding

I never had dreams of marriage because

I grew up with parents who never were

maybe that's why I always chased for love,

maybe that's why I always craved real love

not the love everyone wanted, the love I *needed*.

moonsoulchild

Where I am today is where I prayed to be.

Through everyone wrong one

every anxiety attack

every doubt

every part of myself I couldn't be happy with,

I grew from everything trying to tell me I couldn't.

It's been a long road,

but I'm proud to be here.

Always keep going.

I'm so thankful for your love

because your love taught me

what love is supposed to feel like

your love taught me real love is unconditional

your love taught me,

every other "love" was just a lesson

and your *love*, was *always the answer*.

moonsoulchild

When it's time to part ways with someone
don't keep holding on.
The universe will give you a sign, or many,
which you will choose to overlook
because of "love", but love isn't enough
to hold together what's already broken.
You need to put your heart aside and walk away.

moonsoulchild

I felt strongly about how deep my *love* was

and how far I'd go to prove it,

I lost myself trying to make love work.

Misunderstood to why it wasn't enough

why it wasn't felt. I was vulnerable

how much I had to give, how much I had to prove,

meant more than being *reciprocated*.

moonsoulchild

It wasn't until I filled my own cup

before pouring into another.

The heartache I endured

trying to prove my love

without trying to take care of home first.

Pain was my best friend,

I became good at putting my heart first

without realizing it was a way to become broken.

I feared comfort

the moment I realized

I settled because it was *familiar*

not because it made me happy.

moonsoulchild

"When do you know it's time to let someone go"

When I gave all of me

to the point there was no more to give.

When they didn't question when I became distant.

All the chasing trying to prove my love

when they decided not to chase me back.

Love isn't a choice

you don't "choose" who you love.

Love is a feeling

your hearts way of beating within others

only *your heart can decide* who you love.

moonsoulchild

How much time wasted

trying to make things work that weren't meant to.

All the signs overlooked

when trying to make something make sense

that wasn't meant to.

What's meant for you,

when that time comes

you won't have to think twice, it will just feel right.

moonsoulchild

If you're looking for love

in places it doesn't exist

you can't give love a bad name.

Love doesn't deserve to be lost because you chose

to love someone who didn't love you back.

Love is the reason to keep growing

to find the piece

of whoever deserves to love you.

moonsoulchild

The worst thing you could do,

is let someone make you believe

the love you give isn't enough,

so you keep giving more,

without knowing how consuming it is,

to give all of you

for the need of someone

who doesn't even know your worth.

toxic people are dangerous.

Why fight for a love that only exists within you,

a love that isn't reciprocated back to you?

Why let love blind you

only making love a weapon to you?

You deserve love that exists within you

and within them.

Find the love that doesn't make you feel

like you're difficult to love.

moonsoulchild

After obsessing over my flaws throughout the years,

trying to find someone to love me

while trying to love myself.

I realized,

having flaws didn't mean I was hard to love,

but I deserved a love that didn't give up

because of my imperfections

but love me for them.

If someone doesn't *inspire* you

to be the *best version of you*

they don't love you.

moonsoulchild

I'm at peace knowing who has entered my life

just to tell me they can't stay.

I'm at peace with knowing the person who existed

before I became whole,

is someone I won't repeat.

I have grown

to ever let anything which I let go

turn everything upside down.

When you discover who you are

and how to love you as a whole,

you'll discover love will become unconditional

and not conditional,

and how it feels to *be loved*,

rather than the one always loving.

moonsoulchild

Negative people take a toll on you

even the ones you have loved the most,

sometimes to grow,

you need to let them go,

even if you don't realize they're holding you back.

Don't let people and their trauma,

their burdens,

make you believe you need to take care

of them before you.

moonsoulchild

I remember being lost within lovers

who gave me any ounce of hope

I claimed it as love.

I remember wanting to find love

I created love within ones

who didn't deserve any of me.

I stopped trying to create love, that's when love grew.

I did what I had to,

to let go of the negativity

that was surrounding my life.

I'm proud to say it's no longer following me.

Sometimes it's about forgiving people

when it wasn't your fault

it's making peace for your sake

because your sanity is more important.

Your life matters.

You matter.

Everyday we're thrown something

we might not know how to handle

but it's not the end.

You always have the chance

to make good out the bad.

moonsoulchild

When you fall in love with someone who reciprocates

the same love

someone who takes the time

to understand your soul

and loves you unconditionally,

that's beautiful

and I pray everyone feels this

and not the love everyone believes to be pain.

moonsoulchild

I've loved and lost many times.

I picked up pieces that should have stayed broken.

I ignored the signs.

I chose to overlook one's character because of "love"

and let pain become a reoccurrence.

I let myself become blind to what love was,

I ran with what I made it to be.

moonsoulchild

I remember being someone who wanted to find love,

I created love within people

who didn't have the potential to love me

not even half of what I gave.

I chose to love them.

I chose to give my heart.

I can't blame them

because I thought my love would be enough.

moonsoulchild

Used my heart in situations

where I should have used my head.

I chose love over everything

because love was important.

I didn't know how to condition love

because I couldn't love myself—instead,

I chose to save them,

when I should of chose to be selfish.

moonsoulchild

Someone said

"If I had to choose between me and them

Id always choose them,

I won't ever be selfish and choose myself"

and that spoke to me,

  because they still haven't discovered how important

        they are *choosing you is never selfish.*

If anyone makes you choose,

choose you over them.

Save you,

saving them will only become a war you'll never win.

Toxicity can only consume you

if you allow it to

stop being blind when it's time

open your eyes

moonsoulchild

We all were born to stand out

we all were made beautiful

it just takes years to acknowledge

we don't need to fit in

our beauty comes from within

Even as a work in progress

you should always think of yourself

as the best version of you.

Look at what you've become,

how far you've gotten

always be proud of your growth,

stop beating yourself up

because you're not yet where you want to be.

If someone continues to hurt you

you should think hard

if holding onto them is what's best.

Love isn't strong enough

to hold together what's outgrown.

Love is only strong when it's reciprocated,

if it's not,

you're fighting a battle you'll never win.

moonsoulchild

People will use your mental illness as a weapon

not understanding how weak it makes you.

Some, will bully you until you hit your breaking point

then pray for you when you've hit rock bottom.

It's hard being strong

in a world filled with people

trying to turn you against yourself.

moonsoulchild

You outgrow people you once loved

once you outgrow the you they loved.

We get lost "outgrowing"

we forget there's room for growth

and often confuse growth with change.

If they're not growing with you

you'll outgrow them.

moonsoulchild

We are human,

we make mistakes.

we regret.

we endure pain.

as well as inflicting pain onto others.

we forgive.

we hold on tight.

we let go.

we love,

sometimes too much.

Our hearts are big,

but don't exhaust the way your heart beat

we feel everything because we are human.

moonsoulchild

If it doesn't give my aura the energy it needs,

if it causes me to become miserable

I won't entertain it.

I will leave it

my mental health and my overall energy

isn't going to be anything but taken care of.

I am mature enough to forgive people in this lifetime for the times they treated me less because their insecurities shined brighter. I am mature enough to see the difference in hate, and someone who is just lost. I was once foreign to myself, so if you treated me wrong, under the circumstances, I forgive you. I pray you are at a place in your life where you are happy and at peace, or if you are still soul searching, I pray you are closer to identifying. I am mature enough to know sometimes we love people who were only meant to be a moment.

moonsoulchild

I am mature enough to not hold regrets towards the same people who brought me more pain than love. I am always praying for love, happiness, and peace, for everyone who I loved and lost. Our paths no longer meant to align, while our souls found a deeper connection within. Where we were headed never matched, just like our souls, it only made sense until it no longer did. The love still holds weight over my heart as you will always be remembered, but I am mature enough to know the difference in loving and letting go, and how important to know sometimes you feel both. I am mature enough to admit I held some toxic traits too, and how I let myself be consumed by you. I am mature enough to admit I was not perfect, I brought pain too. I am mature enough to admit to everything you want of me, but I cannot say the same for you, and until then, you will never find peace where you desperately try to.

moonsoulchild

Note to self,

I'm sorry I let you become lost

within the countless times I let you become hurt

over what could have been prevented.

I'm sorry I let you chase people

who didn't care whether you fall behind.

moonsoulchild

A message to best friend who became a memory,

I am sorry it came down to which was more
important, trying to make you love me or saving my
entire being from becoming lost. I am sorry for
leaving you when I promised I never would. I am sorry
I broke so many promises. I am sorry my growth
scared you, and your eyes seen it as change. I am
sorry you could not understand the difference, but
always wanted different. I am sorry you did not love
yourself the way you wanted, so you chose to use my

heart as a place to keep scar. I am sorry you saw me as someone who could be without you, so you chose to push me in that direction. I am sorry you could not find who you were, so you created who you wanted to be, and in the end you never felt whole. I am sorry I could not love you the way you hoped I would. I am sorry you demanded so much, but never thought what I gave was enough. I am sorry I could not be the friend you wanted me to be. I am sorry that I need to love you from afar. I am sorry that the love we once shared became toxic to us. I am sorry my soul will never get to rest without you. I am sorry I always seen the soulmate in you. I am sorry I loved you even when you did not deserve it. I am sorry I still do. Healing from someone you always love, it is crazy, after all this time there is love in my heart for you. But when I noticed your absence brought me peace, I knew one thing for sure,

I was not sorry for choosing me.

Josephine

July 13, 2018 12:34 a.m.

Thank you, Josie. Thank you for being the most amazing angel I could have asked for and though that is the last thing I ever wanted. I never felt as safe as I do, now that I have you by my side. This year has been an experience at the least. But I did things out of my comfort zone and I believe it is because I had you by my side guiding me into the right direction. You always knew what was best, you were the best. But you still are. I hope heaven is as beautiful as you, God is lucky to have you. He is lucky to have someone as wonderful as you. I miss you endlessly. The memories I always have save me from completely losing it. Seeing your face on my phone every time I look at my wallpaper. The love I have for you will never be forgotten. You have given me some of my greatest life moments. You have given me some of the greatest love so pure, so honest. It is hard to capture everything that has happened and to believe you are truly gone. It all still feels like a terrible nightmare. You helped me see the light at the end of the road. You helped me mend my broken heart, even though a piece has left with you. That piece will remain gone, and I will always feel empty when it comes to that piece, until I see you again. Your soul is forever alive, and beautiful Josephine. It is too beautiful to be forgotten, you are too beautiful to be forgotten. I cannot thank you enough for still being wonderful and being the greatest soul mate. I am wishing you a very happy birthday my love. I hope you are doing great up there, I miss you dearly here. But I know you are here. I know you are with us today. We are going to celebrate your beautiful soul. This ones for you baby. Happy 26th birthday Josephine, rock the heavens. I love you, till we meet again, I'll always search for you within the moon,

I know I'll find you there.

moonsoulchild

August 27, 2018 10:30 p.m.

It has been so long. I have not had this kind
of release for over a year, the kind where I lay my
heart out to you because I know you are near, and I
know you hear. Josephine, I miss you so much.
Sometimes I stop and think to myself and remember
your peaceful smile that brought me the kind of joy I
search for within friends I lost in hopes I could fill the
void of you. I try to make friends to fill the void you
took with you, but no one has ever made me
comfortable enough to give my most intimate
thoughts, my deepest secrets, are all with you. I never
felt as safe I do, other than when you are in my
presence, and with you not being here, your spirit is
more alive than you could believe. I feel you very
deeply at this moment and I wish I could just give you
a hug and thank you for being the greatest, most
amazing friend I ever chose to let in. I wish I could see

you one last time to tell you how much I am truly thankful for all the light you brought into my life after all the tragedy. Everything that I been through in the past months have not felt as bad with you by my side guiding me to the part of my life I needed to be. I prayed you were here to see me grow. I prayed you were here to see all my accomplishments, and to see where I am going next. I have found true happiness, and that is all because I had the greatest guardian angel guiding me to the light. I could not have done this without you; your signs, your energy, has gotten me to accept my flaws, because we both know how hard it is to overcome them and loving yourself is a challenge. But you helped me see the importance of self-love, and how amazing it is to be fearless when it comes to loving yourself. How beautiful it feels to be free. I became the free spirit I am with the help of you. Your friendship has saved the parts of me I thought I lost years ago, your friendship saved my sanity. Of course, there is never a day that passes when I ask God if it is possible to see you one last time, but I know we'll meet again, but not under these circumstances. I have come to accept I have you in spirit, and even though you are not whole, you are whole in spirit and always here. You don't miss a moment. I feel you. I find parts of you everywhere. Your soul is the most alive and still as powerful and beautiful as I remember. You guided me to my happiness and never failed me. I tried accepting what fate had in-store for you. I tried to understand why you are gone, but I always come up short.

I have been trying to analyze less and be thankful more that I have you and your friendship is what keeps my soul alive.

moonsoulchild

Death is one of the hardest things

to come to terms with understanding.

it's a huge fear and none of us like facing it.

I had to face the grief up close.

A lot of tears, a lot of praying, and a lot of heart ache.

I had to adapt to understanding

what life after death was

and the spirit that lived on.

There was no time limit

because it's something I'll forever feel,

but I'm at a peace knowing she's still here with me.

moonsoulchild

moonsoulchild

I hope you all

loved this collection

I hope you all

see the growth

thank you all for reading

love y'all

-      Moonsoulchild

moonsoulchild

You can find my work on these platforms:

Instagram: @moonsoulchild

Twitter: @moonsoullchild

Facebook: Moonsoulchild

Made in the USA
Las Vegas, NV
18 February 2022